THE LIFE AND WISDOM OF
TERESA
OF AVILA

THE 'SAINTS ALIVE' SERIES

THE LIFE AND WISDOM OF

TERESA

OF AVILA

Written and Compiled by

LAVINIA BYRNE

Hodder & Stoughton
LONDON   SYDNEY   AUCKLAND

British Library Cataloguing in Publication Data:
A record for this book is available from the British Library.

ISBN 0 340 70969 3

Typeset in Monotype Columbus by
Strathmore Publishing Services, London N7.

Printed and bound in Great Britain by
Mackays of Chatham PLC, Chatham, Kent.

Hodder and Stoughton Ltd,
A division of Hodder Headline PLC,
338 Euston Road, London NW1 3BH

CONTENTS

INTRODUCTION

———◆———

Who are the saints and why should we bother to know about their lives? We are inclined to think of them as heroic people who did extraordinary things, or as people who suffered a great deal and were somehow specially gifted or good. What we then forget is that, in general, saints are people like us. They struggled to know themselves better, to be more kind and loving, more self-accepting, less neurotic. They did not always succeed. They thought their attempts to live with integrity would make them closer to other people and to God. Often what they then discovered was that other people became harder to love and that God simply disappeared.

Yet they kept up the struggle. They believed that they were given one chance, that they had to live with a certain generosity, because this life is a preparation for the full glory of the next life. They then learnt that we are given many chances because all is grace, and the Christian life is a life of grace. So their schemes and plans for being holy were dismantled. All that was asked of them was a readiness to accept the gifts of God, including the final gift of heaven.

Saints come from every walk of life. They are men and women who share our concerns about money, power, politics, peace, energy, food, war, death, sex, love, privacy, the inner life, the outer life, harmony, balance. What makes them distinctive is that they looked beyond themselves to know how best to live and they discovered that God shared their concerns. If we read about them nowadays, we do so out of more than simple curiosity. Their lives are worth reading because we can learn from them. We look for more than a good example, though. The saints seem to know more than we do; they have access to a deeper level of wisdom than our own. They are gurus for our times. So when we read about them, we are quite right to seek an insight into the mind of God, who calls and inspires us all to the heroism of holiness, however we ourselves happen to live. Holiness is for all, not just the few; for a holy life is no more than a life lived in the presence of God.

In our materialistic and agnostic age, do the saints still matter? Have they any wisdom for us, or are they simply a pious irrelevance? A sixteenth-century Spanish nun sounds like an improbable test case. Yet the evidence of her life is astonishingly contemporary as she asks the same questions which still preoccupy us in our own everyday lives.

Teresa of Avila was an adventurous, engaging woman. She knew about passion and she knew about desire. Yet her world stood in judgment over her. It classed her as an outsider. How did she work out her place in the outer world of her family and relationships? How did she choose a way of life which would help her make the human journey towards self-knowledge and self-acceptance with any kind of integrity? How did she learn about her inner world? How did she live and how did she die?

The first part of this book shows how Teresa the gadabout came to understand her own deepest needs. It tells the story of the first half of her life. In the second part, we discover how she learnt to use what she had understood about herself to help other people to know themselves better. Teresa is a Doctor of the Church, a teacher whose lessons about human growth are as fresh and important for our own times as they were for the reform of the Church of sixteenth-century Europe. Part Three gives us a selection of her own prayers and writings.

Teresa of Avila danced to the tambourine and enjoyed a game of chess. She had a wide circle of friends and lost her heart with rare abandon. You could have been forgiven for thinking she was a bit of a butterfly. In the event, as her truest friends realised, you would have discovered that she was something far more interesting. No wonder her most telling images – of an irrigation system, a castle or of the life cycle of a silkworm – tell us all we need to know about human growth and the life of faith.

PART ONE

———◆———

The Story of Her Early Years

Satisfying the soul

PART ONE

Satisfying the soul

It is enough for me to be a daughter of the Catholic Church; for it would trouble me more to have committed a venial sin than to be descended from the lowest and vilest men in the world.

— Letter to Gracían, 1560s

The soul is satisfied with nothing less than God
In 1559, Teresa of Avila described an experience of God's love. She wrote:

I saw an angel close by me, on my left side, in bodily form. He was not large, but small of stature and most beautiful – his face burning, as if he were one of the highest angels, who seem to be all of fire. I saw in his hand a long spear of gold, and at the iron's point there seemed to be a little fire. He appeared to me to be thrusting it at times into my heart and to pierce my very entrails; when he drew it out, he seemed to draw them out also, and to leave me all on fire with a great love of God. The pain was so great that it made me moan; and yet so surpassing was the sweetness of this excessive pain that I could not wish to be rid of it. The soul is satisfied with nothing less than God.

When she died, and was safely buried, the scent from her grave was overwhelming, a blend of clover and some powerful unknown fragrance. Nine months later, her sisters could bear the tantalising evidence no longer. They had the stones, bricks, quicklime and earth removed from over her coffin. This took four days and then they discovered her body was uncorrupt and intact: 'as fresh and whole as if it had been discovered the day before'. Gracián, the man she had loved beyond all the others, was there, in his role as Provincial Superior of the Discalced Carmelites. When her body was stripped and washed and covered with a cloth, he came back to see it. 'Uncovering her breasts,

PART ONE

I was surprised to see how full and firm they were.' Teresa was sixty-eight when she died, a mystic, a poet, the reformer of the Carmelite Order, a woman of passion and fire, a martyr to love.

Who was this woman and how did she come to this extraordinary experience of God's love? How are we to understand her story nowadays? After all, it is not at all normal. She did not enter a convent and live happily ever after, devoted to a quiet hidden life. She had a string of friends and priests in tow and wrote letters to them till three o'clock in the morning. She danced to the sound of a tambourine and played a mean game of chess. She was strong, passionate, wilful, neurotic. She spent the first twenty years of her time in the convent wrestling for a true understanding of herself and of her calling, settled down briefly to the life of a contemplative sister, and then was off on the road again, driven by a vision of what might be. A reformer by nature, she began by reforming herself and then transformed the Church. The story is a complicated one because it is full of unexpected twists. So who was Teresa of Avila and how did she square her certainty that 'the soul is satisfied with nothing less than God' with a life as eventful as her own?

A daughter of the promise

When Teresa Sánchez de Cepeda y Ahumada was born in Avila on 28 March 1515, her true identity was the subject of a cover-up. Her elegant long name suggests that hers was the purest of Spanish aristocratic blood – and that meant a great deal at the time. For Moors and Jews had been expelled from Spain long before her birth, in a drive for racial purity, and to be noble was to be free of what was considered the 'taint' of association with them. Nobility was all and governed by strict rules of convention and breeding. The *hidalgo* or Spanish gentleman was identified as the *hijo* or 'son' *dalgo* 'of someone'.

This was the world into which Teresa was born: a world driven by notions of honour and dignity; a world stripped of the exotic colour and richness which the Moors and Jews had brought to life. The silent courtyards of the former Moorish quarter in Avila no longer rang to

4

the hammer of coppersmiths or artists making inlaid tortoiseshell and mother-of-pearl furniture. Enamels, jewels, silk and stamped leather were no longer created to the sound of falling water from cool fountains. The Jewish quarter was silent too. After their expulsion in 1492, their banking and financial skills, their knowledge of art and medicine had fallen into other hands. Eleven thousand Jews, half the population of the city, had been expelled from Avila alone. To be a Jew was to carry a great stigma. *La limpia sangre* (literally 'clean blood'), which means a kind of ethnic and religious cleansing, was all. This was a Catholic world which claimed to have introduced renewal and reform, yet which stood in need of it at the profoundest religious, human and social level. What kind of God is served on the basis of blood lines, ethnicity and racial or social purity?

Did Teresa herself ever know the absolute sense in which her own place in the reform of the Church and the reform of the religious life was bound up in these questions? As a child, her true identity was veiled from her. When she took the veil, her truest identity before God was revealed to her. The journey was a spectacularly long and difficult one and, almost uniquely among the saints, she wrote her own story with astonishing candour and intelligence. That is why we know so much about her. Nevertheless, histories of Saint Teresa of Avila fall into two collections: those written before 1947 and those written after that date. And Teresa's own is the first of them all, so it too draws a veil over the secrets of her past. The post-1947 literature is different because it has to grapple with a strange revelation, a piece of detective work which appears to fill in gaps in the narrative which now seem inexplicable without it.

The year 1947 saw the publication of an article which claimed to demonstrate that a lawsuit was brought against Teresa's family in 1519 – four years after her birth. There was Jewish blood in Teresa's background. The secret was out. Her grandfather had purchased his elegant name on arriving in Avila. Previously he had lived in Toledo where he was a *converso* or forced convert. The Spanish Inquisition had been brutal. Not only had they demanded his conversion, but subsequently they had caught up with him for some minor infringement of the law and had him beaten with whips and degraded in a public penitential procession around the churches of Toledo. No wonder he had escaped and sought refuge and a new identity in Avila.

His son, Alonso, had witnessed the scene. Aged five, he was old enough to carry the scar of it for the rest of his life. Whether it was carried through to the next generation, none can say, but the humiliation and shame of public exposure in a fanatical culture create wounds which go deep. And the unconscious bears traces of experience which the conscious mind ignores. This is true for individuals but also for families and for nations. The affliction of shame creates intolerable burdens.

In this sixteenth-century Christian culture, there was an added dimension to this burden. To be a Jew, to carry Jewish blood, was to be associated with those who crucified Christ – as the thinking of the time would have had it – and so to carry a double bind. The stigma is a religious as well as a social one. It bites into the heart of an individual's spiritual life. Is there any hope at all? Will true forgiveness ever be possible?

Alonso's father, Juan Sánchez de Toledo, dealt with this as best he could. He bought a letter of nobility in 1500. His six sons bought another one in 1523. A biographer spells out the lie by insisting that this was to 'recover all the privileges and exemptions of the *hidalgos*, lost during the revolt of the *Communidades* against Charles V'. When Alonso married his first wife, Dona Catalina del Peso y Henao in 1504, he bought Avila's former Mint as his residence, the money-house which stood on a hillside near the Church of St Dominic and that of St Scholastica, close by the former Jewish quarter. On the outside he had a coat of arms emblazoned with lions, bezants and ribbons and, eventually, the burning tower of the 'Ahumadas', defended to the last against the Moors. Yet he was a devout man and sought consolation from God in prayer. Teresa herself noted:

My father was a man of much charity to the poor, and compassion for the sick, and even for servants: so much so that he could never be persuaded to keep slaves, for he pitied them greatly; and when a female slave of his brother was in our house he treated her as if she was one of his own children and he said he was so sorry she was not free that he could hardly endure the pain of it. He was of great truthfulness, no one ever heard him swear or murmur. Very pure, too, in everything.

Lives of Teresa written before 1947 could only guess at the reasons for some of the anguish which she wrote about in her own autobiography and the very ambivalence of words like 'pure'. In her biography of Teresa, Vita Sackville-West offered an explanation for the absence of slaves which bore no trace of irony: 'There were no Moorish slaves in the Cepeda palace. Don Alonso, a humane man, disapproved of slaves, so the household was strictly and entirely Spanish.' Those who have written her story since 1947 have grappled with Teresa's anguish as best they can, realising that it may have had complicated origins, being anything but 'entirely Spanish'. The narrative detail or story line is the same in either case. Only the interpretation differs. So who was Teresa Sánchez de Cepeda y Ahumad? And why does her life still matter and hold wisdom and inspiration for us today?

Birth of a reformer

The facts are well documented. So we know, for instance, that she was born in 1515, the daughter of Don Alonso Sánchez de Cepeda by his second marriage to Dona Beatriz de Ahumada, a fourteen-year-old bride. He had had three children by his former wife who died after giving birth to them in rapid succession. When he remarried, he had nine more children, of whom the third was Teresa. When she was thirteen, the little girl's mother died, creating an emotional vacuum in the heart of their family life.

Up to the age of thirteen, Teresa's experience had been little different from that of any other sixteenth-century Spanish child, with one notable exception. Hers was a devout home, so there was daily mass and regular family prayers. She was taught to read early on and borrowed books from a trunk which her mother kept. It was full of saints' lives, romances and tales of heroic exploits and Teresa developed a taste for these. So much so that in 1522, at the age of seven, she persuaded her favourite brother, Rodrigo, to join her on a mission. In the books about saints which she had read, there had been stories of martyrdom. Teresa decided that she and Rodrigo, who was four years older than her, should go off together and convert the Moors, whom she understood to be the enemies of Spain and of true religion. Just like that. Martyrdom would surely follow, but it would be a glorious martyrdom and she and Rodrigo would be numbered among the saints. She chanted a refrain to him: '*para siempre, para siempre, para siempre*'. For ever, for ever, for ever. That is how they would live in heaven, as saints and martyrs with God, assured of glory.

They set off across the river Adaja, bound for the *tierra de Moros*, the land where the Moors live, namely Africa. Half a mile from home they were waylaid and brought home in disgrace by their uncle Francisco who had happened to bump into them on the road. Teresa was punished, though the attraction of journeying never left her. She took up a new game and began to play at being a hermit, building herself a hermitage out of stones in the garden. Whether as martyr or as hermit, she was exploring a relationship with God and with herself. What was her identity? What was her destiny? What was she to be?

The call of the cloister

As a motherless girl in a house full of boys (two older, six younger), with a much older and a much younger sister, Teresa was in fact singled out for a different fate altogether. Her sense of vocation would develop in a more obvious context. At the age of sixteen, she was sent off to school. Her father chose an Augustinian convent of Our Lady of Grace where Teresa stayed eighteen months. One of her teachers, a nun called Maria Brizeno, made a great impression on her and Teresa began to value her friendship. Until now Teresa had not wanted to be a nun at all. She did not terribly want to marry either. She was very pretty and more than a little precocious for she was intelligent and gifted. She had beautiful jewellery, inherited from her mother, and wore it to best effect. Everything conspired to reinforce her sense of honour and of her place in society. She had friends and loved them. Her faults were obvious: a tendency towards vanity and a certain sentimentality. Both, by our own standards, would seem very understandable in a teenage girl, especially one who had lost her mother so young.

Yet Maria told her that 'many are called and few are chosen', making an appeal to Teresa's desire to do something special in God's service and reminding her of the gospel text from Matthew 22. This consoling line of Scripture in fact comes at the end of a horrendous parable, where Jesus has the lord of the banquet give a fierce and apparently arbitrary judgment against one of the guests whom he had called to a wedding banquet. The man had not asked to come, yet once there he was judged and thrown out again:

> When the king came in to see the guests, he noticed a man there who was not wearing a wedding robe, and he said to him, 'Friend, how did you get in here without a wedding robe?' And he was speechless. Then the king said to the attendants, 'Bind him hand and foot, and throw him into the outer darkness, where there will be weeping and gnashing of teeth.' For many are called, but few are chosen. (Matthew 22.11–14)

Teresa's sense of vocation carried with it some of the ambivalence of this story. On the one hand she was glad to be called; on the other she suffered from an excruciating sense of unworthiness. So much so that the cloister repelled her. She knew about her vanity and about her overwhelming need to be loved. She knew that sometimes these led her astray. But her reaction seems immoderate. She fell ill. Her subsequent breakdown and collapse into severe mental as well as physical illness both encourage and repel us. Why should a girl of eighteen have to suffer like this? If God wanted her, why the complications? How could she get some freedom and a sense of her own value? Would the young granddaughter of the *converso* always have to suffer so much?

Convent of the Incarnation

Relief came with a visit to her sister Maria who was married to a man named Martin Guzman. She set off to stay with them at the village of Becedas, breaking the journey briefly at Ortigosa where her uncle Don Pedro lived. Now he was a wise and stabilising influence. He talked calmly to her and gave her a sense of her own true and inner value. She in turn began to look at her call from God more calmly. On her return to Avila, she knew that she would have to become a nun. She chose the Convent of the Incarnation and, without her father's permission, ran away to join the community as once she had run away to convert the Moors.

In November 1536, she set off to join the Carmelite community. Founded in 1478, the

Convent stood in a leafy suburb of Avila with views over trees and gardens. On its original site the buildings had incorporated a former synagogue. The very building itself juggled with the identities which dogged Teresa's past. The sisters' way of life allowed for a relaxed form of cloister and those of Teresa's station in life enjoyed the privilege of private accommodation. She herself had two rooms connected by a staircase, with her bedroom on the second floor and an oratory on the first. The rule was not so severe as that of the earliest Carmelite foundations where the sisters had lived as hermits. Of course there were severe religious disciplines, such as fasting and penance, and the life was a life of prayer. But it could also be a pleasant life, with intelligent companions, interesting visitors and a set of rituals and symbols and shared values which gave Teresa a sense of purpose. She wrote, 'When I took the habit, then the Lord gave me to understand how he favours those who do violence to themselves to serve him, which nobody understood of me, only a great willingness.' There were 180 sisters in the Convent of the

Incarnation at the time, and one of them was a personal friend, Dona Juana Suárez. Once again the human and the divine worked together in Teresa's life. She had a great gift for friendship and her friends gave her a form of companionship and emotional stability which were missing from the very core of her being.

But could she accept such love? Could she accept the very simplicity of the state of life she had chosen? It was not particularly heroic; it was not even particularly hard. So she set off to make it so, outstripping her colleagues and companions with the zeal with which she set about the everyday tasks of religious life.

At first she was wonderfully happy. The life suited her. It played into her desire for instant holiness and gave her the impression that she could gain it just by trying hard. The bitter truth was hard to bear when first it began to dawn on her. For she realised that effort alone could not secure what she most desired, namely union with God.

The effort began to take its toll and the inevitable happened. Once again she became terribly ill. Once again she was shipped off to her sister and brother-in-law at Becedas. And once again she stayed over at her uncle's. Here she was offered relief from a strange source. Just as her childhood reading had given her a sense of vocation and glory, so too a book would now give her a chance to re-think her life. Don Pedro gave her a copy of a spiritual classic, *The Third Spiritual Alphabet,* to read. It was written by a Franciscan called Francesco de Osuna and gave her just the break she needed. Osuna had been a soldier before his conversion and call to the religious life. He was energetic and alive to the need for the spiritual life to engage with people's energy as well as their need for quiet. He advocated an intelligent kind of prayer where God calls us to reason and enquire and to think and meditate. Until then Teresa had been encouraged to say her prayers, to repeat words and get them right. Now she related to God more actively and let her mind wander around the ideas with which she prayed. This offered her huge freedom, but for the moment her over-burdened spirit could not quite take the gift.

At Becedas she became very ill. The symptoms grew worse and worse. Eventually she ended up in a catatonic state, totally immobilised by forces beyond her knowledge and her control. For the rest of her life she would suffer from ill health, but nothing again would ever be so terrible as this experience of incapacity. This was a kind of passion. The tough, proud young woman was being broken in unimaginable ways, so that God could get through her defences. Where would resurrection come?

Return to Avila

She returned to Avila and, as she began to recover, continued to try to pray more reflectively. Gradually her health came back; gradually she began to see that the journey of prayer on which she was embarked could not be accomplished through effort alone. Later she would write most tellingly of the way in which the life of faith and of prayer have to develop gradually.

Hers was an inner journey of distinction. She wrote about it with startling frankness and with imagery which still speaks to the human heart. She lived in an arid landscape, the sun-dried soil of Castile. So she speaks of a garden and how the innermost being can only grow with watering. At first we make a great effort about ourselves, drawing water from a well, as it were, and heaving it about laboriously by our own efforts. Then we learn how to set up systems, waterwheels and buckets which will do the heavy grind for us, but still ensure that we continue to grow. Where there is a stream in the garden though, something new begins to happen. God is actively at work, meandering through our days and watering our souls. But best of all is rain, where we abandon ourselves to refreshment from above and all is grace.

Simple imagery, but a nice description of human striving and where it ends most restfully. In 1544 her father died and Teresa gained an unexpected ally. The priest who had had spiritual care of her father and who had been his confessor came to see Teresa and she realised that she could trust him sufficiently to tell him of her plight. Out of a false sense of humility, she had given up mental prayer, the prayer which most sustained her. For a year and a half she had resisted using it, holding herself back from the call of grace. But now the Dominican priest, Fray Vincente Barrón, encouraged her to take it up again.

Years of transformation

Later she would say that she languished for some twenty years. 'My soul began to grow weary', she wrote, recalling the period before and after her father's death. Without question or doubt, the first twenty years at the Convent of the Incarnation were years of transformation and change, but this change came about slowly. Teresa, the generous young woman who had given herself unreservedly through her own efforts, had to learn to know herself better. At first she raced along, drawing water from a well of her own devising. This made her ill. Then she learnt about water buckets and wheels and systems of irrigation, advancing in the knowledge and love of God through a calmer observance of the Carmelite rule and through the practice of prayer. Nevertheless, she remained troubled throughout this period because she was still haunted by a sense of her own inadequacy and sinfulness. Her gaze was fixed upon herself as well as upon God.

With her father's death and the help of her spiritual director, she gradually became aware of the presence of the river of God's blessing in her life and could pray again more easily, conscious that the stream of grace was meandering through her days.

True transformation came when she was least expecting it. At the end of 1555 there was a special festival at the Convent of the Incarnation. A friend of the community had given the sisters a painting of the crucified Christ. Teresa went into the chapel where it was displayed and began to pray. There followed an experience of grace and of forgiveness which would stay with her to the end of her days. In the presence of her Saviour she could at last let go. All her vanity and self-love and fearfulness fell away. Naked, she came before the naked Christ to be transformed and newly veiled by him.

A convent dedicated to the Incarnation is dedicated to the humanity of Jesus, who is given to the world in trust and love. Teresa had chosen to embrace her own humanity in a safe place like this. Her choice now brought her to a place of abandonment. From now on it would not matter if her blood were pure or not; it would not matter if shame and humiliation were attached to her grandfather and his memory. All that shame was wiped out, it could no longer burden her conscious or her unconscious memory, for she was now watered from above, totally and completely forgiven for every sin or imperfection whether real or imagined. All was grace.

Teresa was now forty years old. She was preparing to enter into her prime. She wrote:

> What a light and a heavy cross you have prepared for those who arrive at this point. Light, because it is sweet; heavy, for there come times when there is no suffering to match it.
>
> May the Lord teach me words so that I can speak about this fourth kind of water. Here one does not have to feel, but to enjoy without

understanding what is enjoyed. This is what they call union, but what it *is*, I cannot make clear. What I wish to explain is what the soul *feels* when she is in this divine union. What union is, that is understood already – it is for two separated things to come together as one. O my Lord, how good you are! You are blessed for ever! May all things praise you, my God, you have loved us so much that we are able to talk truthfully about this communication with us.

Teresa's union with God was not some private possession, a mystical trip between herself and the wounded Jesus. She writes lyrically and poetically about her experience – for she was a poet as well as a writer of prose – but she is also concerned to make the point that those who love God and are loved by God will begin to be selfless. So she ends her reflection on an encouraging note:

For some time this improvement remains in the soul; already, knowing that the fruit of it is not hers, she can start to share it, and this without in any way losing it for herself. She begins to give signs that hers is a soul which holds treasure in heaven, and to have a desire to share it with others, and to beg God that she alone may not be the one who is rich. She begins to do good to those around her, almost without understanding it or taking any account of herself.

A Teresa who takes no account of herself is a Teresa who is free to begin the next stage of her journey, but also a Teresa who lays herself open to attack. There is a fearlessness that goes with being free, and which attracts opposition from more timorous rivals. She would need friends and true support. For this reason, it is all the more astonishing that God appointed Padre Diego de Cetina, a twenty-three-year-old Jesuit scholastic, to be her spiritual director at this juncture. This goes right against the wisdom of our own times. We would be careful to suit the gifts of a Teresa with those of a gifted director. We would hesitate to match such an improbable couple as this. Yet Diego's very inexperience worked in Teresa's favour. He suggested simple remedies and was not at all fazed by the grandeur of this middle-aged Carmelite and her stories of God's dealings with her soul.

When Diego de Cetina died some eleven years later, his superiors sent a private report to Rome in which they dismissed him as 'a mediocre preacher who hears confessions and is fit for nothing else'. Praising with faint damns. Teresa herself had strong words to use about spiritual directors yet would be the first to acknowledge the importance and place of the twenty-two priests to whom she made her confession over the years or who gave her spiritual direction:

It is very important for the director to be a wise man – a man with good understanding and experience; if he is learned too, this will be an advantage. But if you cannot find these three qualities in the same person, the first two are the most important ones, for learned men can be found where necessary. I do not mean that beginners should not have the opportunity to communicate with learned people, for I should prefer spirituality to be unaccompanied by prayer than not to be founded upon the truth. Learning is a great thing, for it teaches those of us who have little knowledge, and gives us light, so that, when we are faced with the truth of holy scripture, we act as we should. From foolish devotions may God deliver us!

My opinion has always been, and always will be, that every Christian should try to consult some learned person, and the more learned this person, the better. Those who walk in the way of prayer have a great need of learning and the more spiritual they are, the greater is their need.

Of Diego de Cetina, Teresa herself wrote:

He left me consoled and strengthened, and the Lord helped me through him, and helped him to understand my condition and how to direct me. I remained determined not to depart from what he commanded me in anything, and so

have I done to this day. Praised be the Lord,
who has given me grace to obey my confessors,
though imperfectly; and almost always they
have been of those blessed men of the Society
of Jesus.

Her dilemma had been solved. Before her
father's death, she had stopped praying in the
way she found most attractive and helpful, and
now could begin again. Instead of being tied
into the ritual recitation of vocal prayers, she was
free to pray with her mind and to risk true
encounter with God. So why had she stopped
praying in the first place? The answer is not a
particularly complicated one, but it is an alarm-
ing one. Not only was the Council of Trent
(1545–63) organising the renewal of the wider
church, but Teresa's Spain was something of a
religious minefield in its own right. The intro-
duction of an Index of Prohibited Books in 1559
would be a case in point.

For the Spanish Inquisition, having worked
against the Jews and the Moors, now brought
conflict into the heart of church life. Founded in

1479, it would only be suppressed in 1820 and during that period, it created and rooted out innumerable enemies. While it successfully nipped in the bud the development of any form of Spanish Protestantism, it also generated suspicion and hostility on an unparalleled scale. No one was beyond the long arm of the law.

Religious extremism was characteristic of the reform of the Spanish church, so where did Teresa stand? Was she an *alumbrada*, a visionary, an *illuminata*, and so an enemy of true religion? Was she on the side of the *letrados* – or learned theologians – or on the side of the *espirituales* – those who believed in spirituality and a spiritual approach to God? She had grown afraid of the power of her own mysticism because it called into question her loyalty to the system. If she thought hers was *limpia sangre*, then her sense of family honour was such that she assumed her loyalty should be given without question. If she knew it was not, or suspected that somehow her identity was flawed at its very core, then she had a further problem. The burden of proof always lay with her.

What a blessing therefore to reach the stability and freedom of her middle years. She could abandon the burden of trying to prove who she was and how close to God she could become. Instead she was to enjoy what she called 'another and a new life': 'From this point onward, I am speaking of another and a new book – I mean of another and a new life. Until now the life I was describing was my own; but the life I have been living since I began to expound these matters concerning prayer is the life which God has been living in me – or so it seemed to me.'

The next stage of Teresa's journey was about to begin. With it came a release of her natural gifts and graces and abilities. She would change the face of the Church in Spain – and beyond – through her renewal of the life and faith of her community. Having herself been called to the true glory of intimacy with God, she would now share the fruits of her call. She was to demonstrate what it means to claim that her soul was 'satisfied with nothing less than God'.

PART TWO

The Wisdom of Teresa

The life of the spirit

PART TWO

The life of the spirit

> Do not mention her name! She is a disobedient contumacious woman who promulgates pernicious doctrine under the pretence of devotion; leaves her cloister against the orders of her superiors and the decrees of the Council of Trent; is ambitious and teaches theology as though she were a doctor of the Church, in contempt of St Paul who commanded women not to teach.
>
> – *The Papal Nuncio*

The call to faith: Teresa the mystic
Teresa offered another reason to explain why she had stopped praying in the years before her father died. Her convent was too noisy. With so much coming and going, so many visitors, so much stimulation from the outer world, the convent was not serving its purpose in her life. It was

preventing her from true contact with God rather than securing it. Other commentators have added wryly that it was not simply the convent which was at fault; Teresa's whole life was so busy and so full of crowds of friends and relations that God could not get a word in edgeways. The serene still centre at the heart of her life was somehow not accessible to her and so she was not able to pray as she might. This is a consoling message. Teresa was a raging extrovert; she was both drawn to and repelled by the life of prayer. She was an intellectual woman, someone who was more persuaded by a telling argument, than by a bid to her feelings. If anything, her feelings persecuted her, for there she was weak and undefended, a prey to emotions which she could not control. God got at her through her feelings and called her to journey to new insights and certainties. So Teresa is able to teach us that prayer is elusive. When we observe her, we discover that one of the Church's greatest mystics had a problem with it, because she was undergoing a great life change.

Prayer is not easy. It is not simply about

relaxing with God, or letting grace sweep over one. It is about the whole orientation of a life, taking us as we are and delivering us to a place where we might not otherwise venture. It fixes the prayerful individual on perspectives which go beyond the end of human life. Most of us are terrified of prayer because it reminds us of death. True contemplation is the closest most of us get to the experience of dying, for our systems shut down and we are taken to a place of haunting silence and incapacity. How much easier it is to get on with the business of living, with snatched conversations with God and a quick read from the Bible to see us on our way.

We prefer to hang on to our anxieties and neuroses, our pains and longings and loves, our sufferings and our griefs. For if we hang on to them, we have a sense of being able to control their outcome. Nothing feels so bad as letting go and letting God embrace us with our distress or joy. Yet this is precisely what Teresa did and it turned her life around.

God confirmed her choice with a series of visions, ecstasies and raptures. The most striking account is of the visit of the angel with the dart of love, piercing her very heart, assuring her that her soul would be 'satisfied with nothing less than God'. Her sisters told of her tendency to levitate, to be lifted physically from the ground as she received communion or as she prayed. Teresa herself writes in a matter-of-fact way about these extraordinary visitations. Hers was to be an increasingly practical mysticism. In one of her letters, she wrote:

Jesus be with you. I said in the letter that went with the Alba courier that the sardines had arrived in good condition and that the sweets had duly arrived too, though I had rather you had kept the best ones. May God reward you.

It is well with us both just now. What great things the Lord is doing! He seems to be pleased to show forth his greatness in raising up wretched creatures and doing us all these favours – and I know of none more wretched than you and I. I must tell you that, for over a week, I have been in such a condition that, if I were to go on, I should hardly be able to attend to all my business. Since I wrote to you I have had the raptures again, and they have been most distressing. Several times I have had them in public – during Matins, for example. It is useless to resist them and they are impossible to conceal. I get so dreadfully ashamed that I feel I want to hide away somewhere. I pray God earnestly not to let them happen to me in public: will you make this prayer for me too, for it is an extremely awkward thing and I don't believe my prayer is any better for it? Latterly I have been going about almost as if I were drunk; but at least it is clear that the soul is well employed, for, as the faculties are not free, it is a grievous thing for the soul to have to occupy itself with anything save the object of its desire.

Previously, for nearly a week, I have been in such a state that I could hardly think a single good thought, so severely was I suffering from aridity.

The blend of sardines and raptures is a typical one, for Teresa did not stop being interested in food and clothes and houses when she undertook the reform of the Carmelite Order. This insight into the working of her mind is refreshing. Great gifts in prayer did not make her inhuman, they made her more human, and that is why any study of her mysticism has to be embodied. It has to notice what was happening in her outer life as well as learning from her of the inner workings of her soul. For when we concentrate on someone's inner life, we can be deluded into believing that that is where all the action is. In Teresa's case this is patently not true. She confuses our categories about what it is to be a mystic, for her inner and outer worlds mirrored each other, and neither can be understood without the other.

The call to hope: Teresa the reformer

Teresa claimed that her convent was too noisy, and so she set about making a new convent. She planned and plotted and persevered. From 1560, the year after the visit from the angel with the dart of love, to 1567, she enjoyed the happiest years of her life. There were still friends. Indeed, she could not have founded her new convent of

St Joseph without the help and intervention of her dearest friend, Dona Guiomar de Ulloa. She wrote of her that they were 'closer than if they had been sisters', as she had spent so much time with her. There were still confessors and directors and Jesuits and Carmelites and Dominicans galore – and Jerónimo Gracían, the great love of her life, had yet to emerge. They first met in 1575.

But Teresa had a task and she set about it with fervour and enthusiasm. From 1560 to 1563, she plotted the launch of her new convent. It was to be dedicated to St Joseph, a saint to whom she had a great devotion. For the Christ child had had to be obedient to Joseph, just as Teresa had now to be obedient to the will of God. The venture was not without problems. Teresa was planning to launch her new project in Avila itself. Was this entirely tactful? How would the other sisters at the Convent of the Incarnation feel as one of their own company took off into a reformed way of life, wiping the proverbial dust off her shoes as she went? Her choice was a judgment on theirs. Equally, there was a problem about money. Teresa had no cash resources for her project. Avila was already stiff with religious houses. Could the faithful be relied upon to support her venture – and should they?

In the event the move to St Joseph's was achieved relatively calmly. Another of her friends, the saintly Peter of Alcántara, had secured papers from Rome which gave the convent a degree of independence. It was to be under the jurisdiction of the Bishop, rather than of the Carmelite fathers. When the house was being set in order, her brother-in-law had fallen ill. She used the house as an infirmary to offer him space for his convalescence, whilst overseeing the work of the builders and the completion of the premises. The convent was inaugurated with a special mass on 24 August 1562 and four sisters were clothed with the habits which Teresa had made for them. They put on the *alpargatas*, the hemp-soled sandals which marked them off as Discalced, or shoeless, Carmelites. Her vision was now fleshed out. The reform of Carmel had begun.

Money problems dominated the first year
and Teresa herself was not able to join the community until the following summer. Yet once she
got there, she began to enjoy a sense of renewal
and purpose which had evaded her for years.
The great hierarchies of the Convent of the
Incarnation were put behind her; at St Joseph's
her sisters had a shared honour, based on their
shared life. In this new convent there would be
no privileges, marking out one sister as better or
more noble than another. Theirs was to be a
common life, in the best sense of the word.
There could be no hangers-on either, for there
would be no space for them. Teresa was
insistent:

> Those who build large houses have their own
> reasons for doing so and are led by religious
> motives, but any corner does for thirteen poor
> women. If there should be any grounds (as
> there must be, on account of the enclosure and
> because they are a help to prayer and devotion),
> by all means let there be hermitages in which to
> retire for prayer, for weak human nature

requires some indulgence; but let the convents
be neither large nor handsome.

Teresa was now forty-nine and would spend
her fiftieth birthday at the heart of a small and
devout community, secure in the knowledge and
love of God, secure too in her own identity. She
thought that she had arrived.

The evidence goes against this claim, for over
the next eighteen years this pattern would be
repeated sixteen times. She simply could not sit
still. The journey of the second half of her life
did not see her a changed person; it re-directed
her energies and gave them a new focus. In 1567,
the travel bug which had sent the child Teresa off
in pursuit of the Moors got hold of her again.
Teresa hit the road. She went to found a new
community in Medina del Campo. This was the
first of an exhausting series of journeys which
would take her from Malagón to Valladolid, from
Salamanca to Seville, from Caravaca to Toledo
and eventually to Alba de Tormes where she
would die in 1582. Her foundations flourished,
the religious and spiritual life of the Church was

renewed through them. But what of Teresa herself? How was she personally renewed as she set about the renewal of the Carmelite Order?

The call to charity: Teresa and her friends

In 1568 Teresa met the twenty-five-year-old friar, Juan de la Cruz. St John of the Cross, as we know him, became the first of the Carmelite men to answer Teresa's call to a return to their strict rule of life and observance. He would suffer terribly at the hands of the Calced Friars, for his fervour invited the charge of heresy. In 1577 he was kidnapped by them and incarcerated in Toledo for nine months. They put him in a box-like cell, a small space some ten feet by six feet, with a diet of bread and water. He wrote some of his greatest poetry in this confined space, poetry of passion and desire which cast him totally on the mercy of God, the divine lover.

Persecution was inevitable, because a reformer stands in judgment over what is reformed. Persecution was inevitable in a country which found tolerance so difficult. When the Jews were first sent out of Spain in 1492, they were allotted four months to quit the country. Two hundred thousand people were sent packing. In Teresa's own times, the work of the Inquisition had led to wholesale destruction by fire of the opposition, the *auto-da-fé*. This was brutal, intransigent reform. Teresa's desire to renew the religious life was based on consent and holy desires. She wanted people to be drawn to God, not forced into sudden conversion. The granddaughter of the *converso* would not wish to violate people's feelings, however passionate her own desires. No wonder she attracted pious, generous companions like John of the Cross. No wonder another young man, Jerónimo Gracían, would be drawn to her.

In 1571 Teresa returned to the Convent of the Incarnation, this time as prioress. Her work as reformer had not gone unopposed. She was now sixty and she was tired. To be asked to come back to the place where she had first begun and to implement the reforms of the religious life which she had seen work so beneficially elsewhere was a burden for her. Yet she set out to do it to the best of her power.

Four years later, whilst founding another house at Beas, she met with Gracían, a young man of thirty. He was a brilliant young academic, a diplomat and a priest. They were immediately attracted to each other and found a depth of spiritual compatibility based on human love of a high order.

Teresa had always had and needed friends. Even when she put her life on to a new under-standing by moving from the Incarnation to St Joseph's she had recognised that friends are indispensable. She sought out the quiet of St Joseph's and what it represented. The irony is that with that kind of silence at the heart of her life, a silence which enabled her mystical gifts to flourish, she could now embrace the most pre-cious gift of all, a companion who was half son, half brother, half lover, with all the contradic-tions that implies. Where John of the Cross had met her soul, Gracían could meet her mind. Their companionship meant everything to her. Later Gracían would write, 'The love I had for Mother Teresa and she for me produced in me purity, ardour and love of God, and in her, comfort and relief in her work as she often told me, and so I loved no one, not even my mother, more than her.'

Her writings

Gracían kept all his letters from Teresa in a specially bound book. She was an extraordinary correspondent, scribbling away at letters way into the night. She used to say that she was sorry she could not write with both hands at once, dashing off a couple of notes simultaneously. Her handwriting is strong and regular. She dispenses with niceties like punctuation, preferring a slash sign at the end of sentences. This is true of her books as well as her letters. There are three of them and each dates from a significant period in her own life.

The first is the *Life,* or autobiography. Teresa wrote this in 1562, the year before she finally moved into the Convent of St Joseph. It is a frank account of her life from childhood to the age of forty-eight. Teresa writes with two deliberate intentions. One is to set out the facts and to give an account of her story. The other is altogether more subtle: she is concerned to demonstrate that she is a loyal daughter of the Church and not some folksy kind of character belonging to a spiritual or heretical sub-class. So she tells her story with all its ups and downs, addressing her text to her confessor, Father García de Toledo. By making a clean slate, she seeks to dispel rumours or conjecture about herself. This is one reason why the manuscript is so frank and why its language and imagery are so plain and authoritative.

In 1567 she completed *The Way of Perfection*, her account of the growth of the spiritual life. This time she takes up her story at the point of the foundation of her own convent at St Joseph's. On the title page she set out her intention:

This book contains advice and counsel given by Teresa of Jesus to her sisters and daughters, the religious of the convents which, with the help of our Lord and the glorious Virgin Mother of God, our Lady, she has founded according to the Primitive Rule of our Lady of Carmel. It is specially dedicated to the sisters of the Convent of St Joseph, Avila, the first of her houses in which, while Prioress there, she wrote this treatise.

So the book is to be a treatise, that is to say, it is meant to help the sisters in her convents to pray. Part of it gives information about the spiritual life, explaining God's ways with the individual soul. She writes about food and hunger, about the importance of good example, about distractions in prayer, about health and friendship, family ties and perseverance. She writes about growth in the knowledge and love of God and above all, about the need for humility. Teresa was adamant: neither Martha nor Mary is superior, both are needed.

Saint Martha was holy, but we are not told that she was a contemplative. What more do you want than to be able to grow to be like that blessed woman, who was worthy to receive Christ our Lord so often in her house, and to prepare meals for him, and to serve him and perhaps to eat at table with him? If she had been absorbed in devotion all the time, as the Magdalen was, there would have been no one to prepare a meal for this Divine Guest. Now remember that this little community is Saint Martha's house and that there must be people of all kinds here. Nuns who are called to the active life must not murmur at others who are very much absorbed in contemplation, for contemplatives know that, though they themselves may be silent, the Lord will speak for them, and this, as a rule, makes them forget themselves and everything else.

Remember that there must be someone to cook the meals and count yourselves happy in being able to serve like Martha. Reflect that true humility consists to a great extent in being ready for what the Lord desires to do with you and happy that he should do it, and in always considering yourselves unworthy to be called his servants. If contemplation and mental and vocal prayer and tending the sick and serving in the house and working at even the lowliest tasks are of service to the Guest who comes to stay with us and to eat and take his recreation

with us, what should it matter to us if we do one
of these things rather than another?

Part of *The Way of Perfection* is an extended
reflection on the Lord's Prayer, offering inspiration in the form of a commentary. This gives us
a sense of how Teresa herself first learnt to pray,
how she allowed her mind to come to understanding by letting it savour the words she was
using. Even the most familiar of words, such as
those of a well-loved prayer, she argues, can open
out and blossom when they are used for spiritual
reflection in this way.

In 1577 she wrote what is arguably her greatest work. *The Interior Castle* tells the awesome
story of the journey of the soul. This is the
mature Teresa sharing her insights and the full
wisdom of her journey in prayer. She sees a
castle in her imagination, with different rooms
which lead through into a central chamber
where God lives and union with God is realised.
The first of these rooms or mansions is about
the drama of self-discovery and self-knowledge.
The soul becomes alert to the possibility of

journeying. This is a crucial moment: where is this journey to be made? For the first twenty years of Teresa's own life she had lived on the outside of herself, assuming that the spiritual life was about journeying towards some distant goal. The childhood experience of looking for Moors to convert in some remote land was always a powerful metaphor in her life. Only in her middle years did Teresa come to understand that the truest journey is that which we undertake towards the core of our being.

To realise this is to come to the second mansion, to be lit up by the desire for prayer and conversation with God. This means a kind of conversion, a turning about on ourselves so that we begin to face inwards rather than outwards. Christ is revealed to us and seeks us out, leading us towards the third mansion where we are called to a life of virtue. Teresa now notes that many people live their entire spiritual lives at this point. They get stuck in the third mansion which, while being a wholly admirable place, is nevertheless quite comfortable. It is a place of virtue and many virtuous people become complacent. They fail to take the risk of another journey. Yet the fourth mansion beckons. It is a place of transition, for here human effort becomes transformed by God's grace. God takes over the life of the soul, just as, in her earlier example, the river in the dry garden takes over the work of the water carrier or our own irrigation systems. The prayerful person now moves from a spiritual life based on effort and action to one based on receptivity. Prayer becomes more passive: God's work, not our own.

In the fifth mansion the soul feels as though it is asleep, enjoying the prayer of passive recollection, a sweet openness to the will of God and tender rest. There is a death and it is the death of understanding which now surrenders itself into the understanding of God. Her image of the silkworm, and the way it grows through changing often, is among the most memorable of any she uses, and prepares us for life in the next mansion. For the sixth mansion too brings a kind of death with it, as here the will lets go and the soul is besieged by raptures, ecstasies and trances. Teresa writes from her own experience as she tries to reassure the prayerful person that these spiritual phenomena, while unusual, are not totally terrifying. She teaches discernment, how to tell what is true from what is false, how to be led towards God and away from the sources of evil. All is gift and grace as the soul makes its way towards the innermost mansion of all, the place of true encounter and union with God. Here in the seventh mansion there is a strange forgetfulness of all that went before. The death or release of memory secures the presence of the soul in God, God in the soul.

This was to be Teresa's own experience as she too arrived at the state of union with God which she so much craved. The journey had been a long one. There had been so many starts: the conversion of the Moors, the building of little hermit huts as a child; the friendships of her teenage years – even ones for which she later berated herself, as they led her into vanity; the first stab at the religious life at the Convent of the Incarnation; her sickness and the full traumas of her constant ill-health; her friendships, including those with some of her more colourful friends like the one-eyed Princess of Eboli – a character who gave Teresa something of a run for her money; the foundation at St Joseph's and years of serenity that followed it; and then the road again as she trundled across Spain in a covered wagon, saying her prayers and berating God for the hard time she was having, as she set about the renewal of Carmel; the chaplains, confessors and directors who lent her their support; the younger men, John of the Cross, the beloved Gracían; the enemies, the opposition, the harsh words of the Papal Nuncio; her struggles with the king to get John out of prison; the welter of experiences and insights which formed her and which gave her such a rich and colourful life, albeit from behind the veil she had chosen.

In the end this veil would be raised and her writings would establish Teresa not simply as a mystic and a saint, but also as a Doctor of the Church. For nothing could conceal the work of God in the life of Teresa of Avila, daughter of the Church and reformer *extraordinaire*.

PART THREE

Prayers and Writings

PART THREE

———————◆———————

Prayers and Writings

Use these prayers to pray with Teresa of Avila. All the great themes of the saint's spiritual journey are here: her trust in God and longing for union; her growing under- standing that the real journey she has to make is an inward one; her distrust of worldly honours and a cul- ture of pride; her longing for heaven and for the renewal of the religious life of her sisters. The language may sometimes seem antique, but the spiritual inspiration behind the words is not. Above all, value the image of the silkworm and take inspiration from it for yourself.

A prayer naming and praising God

O Thou our Monarch!
King of glory, Lord of lords,
Sovereign of all princes, Chief among the Saints!
O Power, dominating over all else!

Wisdom above all knowledge, having neither
  beginning nor end!
Limitless in all Thy works, which are infinite and
  incomprehensible
and a fathomless abyss of wonders!
O Beauty containing all other beauty!
Thou art strength itself; Thou art the truth, O
  Lord, and the genuine riches:
do Thou reign for ever!
Most merciful God! would that I possessed the
  combined eloquence of all the human race,
  with wisdom to understand – as far as the
  understanding can attain in this life, which is
  but utter ignorance – that I might succeed in
  telling at least a few of the many things that
  might be pondered over, in order to obtain
  some feeble idea of the perfections of this our
  Lord and only Good.

                                    – *The Way of Perfection*

Extracts from Teresa's reflection on the Lord's Prayer

Our Father who art in heaven

You have a good Father given you by the holy Jesus: let no other father be known here through any words of yours. Strive, daughters, to merit God's caresses; cast yourselves into His arms. You know that He will never send you from Him while you remain dutiful children. Who would not guard against losing such a Father? Ah, what a consolation this is! Still, rather than enlarge on the subject, I prefer to leave it to your own thoughts, for, however inconstant your imagination may be between such a Son and such a Father, the Holy Spirit must perforce be found. May He inflame your will and constrain you with most fervent love, since even your own great gain suffices not to urge you to it.

Do you suppose it is of little consequence whether or not you know what this heaven is, and where you must seek your most holy Father? I assure you that it is most important for restless minds not only to know this but to realise it by experience, for it is a most efficient means of concentrating the thoughts, and of recollecting the soul. You know that God is everywhere, which is most true. Now, the place in which the king dwells is called his court: so, wherever God dwells, there is heaven, and you may feel sure that all which is glorious is near His Majesty.

Remember what St Augustine tells us – I think it comes in his *Meditations;* how he sought God in many places and at last found the Almighty within himself. It is of no slight importance for a soul given to wandering thoughts to realise this truth, and to see that it has no need to go to heaven in order to speak to the eternal Father or to enjoy His company: nor is it requisite to raise the voice to address Him, for He hears every whisper however low. We are not forced to take wings to find Him, but have only to seek solitude and to look within ourselves.

Hallowed be thy name; Thy kingdom come
The good Jesus bids us say these words which ask that this kingdom may come in us –

'Hallowed be Thy name; Thy kingdom come.'
How great is the wisdom of our Master and our
Spouse! It is well that we should all learn what
we ask for when praying for this kingdom. His
Majesty knew that, unless He enabled us to do so
by giving us His kingdom here on earth, our
natural defects would render us unfit either to
hallow, praise, magnify, glorify, or extol the holy
name of the eternal Father. The good Jesus therefore placed the two petitions close together. I
will tell you what I understand about the matter,
that you may realise what you are praying for,
how eager we should be to gain it, and how we
should strive to please Him Who can give
it to us.

Among the many other joys, the principal
happiness of heaven appears to me to consist in
a disregard of all earthly things and in a peace
and glory that dwell in a soul which rejoices in
the bliss of its companions. It lives in perfect
peace.

Thy will be done on earth as it is in heaven
Let us now learn what Christ offers God on our

behalf and what He wishes us to give His Father in return. We must first see what our Lord requests of us, for it is only right that we should do Him some service in acknowledgment of such supreme blessings. O good Jesus ! whilst demanding so much for us, how little dost Thou give in return – how little, I mean, on our part – for it is as nothing compared with the debt we owe this mighty Monarch. And yet, my Lord, Thou hast not left us without means of repaying Him, for we give all we can if, when we say the words, 'I wish that as Thy will is done in heaven so it may be done on earth,' we yield Him our wills.

Thou hast done well, O our good Master! in making this petition come last, so that we may be able to accomplish what Thou dost promise for us here. For truly, O Lord, hadst Thou not done so our task would have seemed hopeless; yet, since Thy Father bestows His kingdom on us at Thy prayer, I know that we can fulfil Thy promise by giving what Thou didst offer in our name. For since my 'earth' is now made 'heaven' it is possible for Thy will to be done in me; otherwise, in 'earth' so barren and so wretched, I know not how it could have come to pass. For Thou askest so great a thing.

There are many souls (and I was among their number) whom God moves to devotion and visits with holy inspirations and light to know the worthlessness of all earthly things, and on whom He finally bestows His kingdom in this prayer of quiet. Yet these souls close their ears against Him because they prefer to speak and to hurry through a number of vocal prayers as if a task has been set them to say a certain amount every day. Thus when our Lord puts His kingdom into their possession by means of the prayer of quiet and interior peace, they will not accept it, but think they can do better by reciting prayers which distract their attention. Do not imitate them, my sisters, but be attentive when God gives you this grace; think what a priceless treasure you would lose, and be assured that you had far better say one petition of the Pater Noster from time to time than repeat the whole prayer mechanically and hurriedly over and over again. He to Whom you speak is very near you – He cannot fail to hear, and I believe that in this way we truly praise and hallow His name. Now that you are the inmates of His house, you glorify Him with stronger love and desire; indeed, it seems as if you could not choose but serve Him. I advise you to be very careful about this, as it is of the utmost importance.

So great is the gift that our good Master has asked for us and has taught us to beg for ourselves, that it includes all we can desire in this life.

Give us this day our daily bread

Seeing our needs, the good Jesus found a most wonderful way by which to prove His excessive love for us – in His own and in His brethren's name He made this petition: Give us this day our daily bread, O Lord! For the love of God, daughters, let us realise the meaning of these words: our spiritual life depends on our not disregarding them.

Reckon as of little value whatever you may have given to God in comparison with this rich reward. It appears to me, although I submit my opinion to a higher judgment, that though the good Jesus knew what an advantage it would be for us to yield to His Father what He had offered on our behalf, yet He recognised the obstacles to our keeping our promise that come from our human nature, its tendency to degradation, and our want of love and courage. He saw that there was need to aid and encourage us, and this, not once for all, but day by day, therefore He determined to remain among us.

And forgive us our trespasses as we forgive those who trespass against us

What value God places on our loving and keeping peace with one another! For when once we have given Him our will we have given Him the right to it, and this we cannot do without love. See, sisters, what need there is for us to love and to agree with each other. The good Jesus places it before anything else. He does not mention the many things we gave Him on one single occasion, nor does He offer them in our name to His Father. He might have said: 'Forgive us because of our many penances, or prayers, or fasts, or because we have left all for Thee and love Thee fervently, and have suffered for Thee and long to suffer more.' He never says: 'Because we would lay down our lives for Thee', or recounts the many other things the soul does for God when it loves Him and gives Him its will. He only pleads: 'As we forgive our debtors'. Perhaps this was because He knew of our attachment to this miserable 'honour', so that we will overlook no slight upon it. This being the most difficult thing for us to overcome, our Lord put it in the first place, so that, after having asked such sublime graces for us, He offers this for our repayment.

Notice, sisters, that Christ says, 'As we have forgiven our debtors', to show that it is a thing we have already done, as I said. Be sure of this – when a soul, after receiving some of the special favours in prayer which I have described and after having been raised to perfect contemplation, does not come away with a firm determination to forgive others, and if occasion offers, does not actually pardon any injury, serious as it may be – unless these fruits are left in the soul, the graces never came from God but were illusions and delights caused by the devil to make such a person think herself holy and therefore worthy of greater honour. I am not speaking of the trifles people call injuries, for these do not affect a soul that God raises to so high a prayer, nor does it care whether it is highly esteemed or no. I am wrong in saying that it does not care, for honour troubles it far more than contempt, and it dislikes rest much more than toil. The good Jesus, knowing that these results remain in the soul that has reached this state of prayer, assures His Father that we forgive our debtors, for when God has really given His kingdom to a person she no longer wishes for any kingdom in this world: she understands that this is the way to reign in a far higher manner, experience having taught her what benefit accrues from it and that the soul makes rapid progress through suffering for God.

And lead us not into temptation
Always try to be humble, sisters; believe that you are unworthy of these gifts and do not seek them. I am convinced that in this way the evil one loses many a soul which he thought to have ruined, and that our Lord draws good out of the harm the fiend meant to work us, for His Majesty looked at

our intention, which is to serve and please Him by keeping in His presence in prayer, and He is ever faithful. But we must be cautious, lest the enemy make a breach in our humility by vainglory: and we must beg God to preserve us from this. Then you need not fear, daughters, that he will allow any one but Himself to console you for long.

But deliver us from evil
It would be hopeless, sisters, to suppose that while we are on earth we can be freed from numberless temptations, imperfections, and even sins, since Holy Scripture says: 'If we say that we have no sin, we deceive ourselves.' This is the truth. Then, if we flee from bodily evils and sufferings – and who is without many a trial of the sort? – is it not right to ask to be delivered from the ills of the soul? Still, we must recognise that it is impossible for us to be delivered from every corporal evil or from imperfections and faults in God's service. I am not speaking of the saints – they 'can do all things in Christ' as St Paul said, but of sinners like myself. When I see how engulfed I am in my own weakness, tepidity,

want of mortification, and other faults, I feel the need of asking God for some redress. As for you, daughters, pray for what you think best: I shall never be free from these evils in this life and so I beg to be delivered from them in eternity. What good do we possess on earth, where we are destitute of all good and absent from our Lord? Deliver me, O God! from this deadly nightmare; deliver me from the many labours, the frequent anguish, the numberless vicissitudes, the multitude of duties that devolve upon us in this world: from the many, many, many things that harass and that weary me, and that would weary any reader of this book were I to enumerate them. Life is made unbearable by the loathing I feel at having led so bad a life and at the sight of its unworthiness even now, considering my indebtedness.

Therefore I beg of God to deliver me for ever from all evil since I cannot pay the score I owe, but, perhaps, only plunge deeper into debt each day. O God! Unbearable are the uncertainties as to whether I love Thee or whether my desires are pleasing to Thee. My Lord and my God! Deliver me from all evil and vouchsafe to take me to where all good things are to be found. What do souls look for here, after Thou hast shown them in some degree the nothingness of this world, or when they have learnt it by experience, and have a lively faith in what the eternal Father is keeping in store for us because His Son asked Him to bestow it on us and has bidden us beg it for ourselves?

An ardent and constant desire for heaven is a sure sign in contemplatives that the favours they receive come from God and that their contemplation is genuine, for He is drawing their souls to Him. So let those who possess it value it highly. But let nobody suppose that I ask for heaven for this reason – it is only because my life has been so wicked that I am afraid of living any longer – besides, I am tired of bearing so many crosses.

Amen

Blessed and praised be God, from Whom comes all the good that we either speak, or think, or do! Amen.

– Extracts from *The Way of Perfection*

You have heard how wonderfully silk is made – in a way such as God alone could plan – how it all comes from an egg resembling a tiny peppercorn. Not having seen it myself, I only know of it by hearsay, so if the facts are inaccurate the fault will not be mine. When, in the warm weather, the mulberry trees come into leaf, the little egg which was lifeless before its food was ready, begins to live. The caterpillar nourishes itself upon the mulberry leaves until, when it has grown large, people place near it small twigs upon which, of its own accord, it spins silk from its tiny mouth until it has made a narrow little cocoon in which it buries itself. Then this large and ugly worm leaves the cocoon as a lovely little white butterfly.

If we had not seen this, but had only heard of it as an old legend, who could believe it? Could we persuade ourselves that insects so utterly without the use of reason as a silkworm or a bee would work with such industry and skill in our service that the poor little silkworm loses its life over the task? This would suffice for a short meditation, sisters, without my adding more, for you may learn from it the wonders and the wisdom of God. How if we knew the properties of all things? It is most profitable to ponder over the grandeurs of creation and to exult in being the brides of such a wise and mighty King.

Let us return to our subject. The silkworm symbolises the soul which begins to live when, kindled by the Holy Spirit, it commences using the ordinary aids given by God to all, and applies the remedies left by Him in His Church, such as regular confession, religious books, and sermons; these are the cure for a soul dead in its negligence and sins and liable to fall into temptation. Then it comes to life and continues nourishing itself on this food and on devout meditation until it has attained full vigour, which is the essential point, for I attach no importance to the rest. When the silkworm is full grown, as I told you in the first part of this chapter, it begins to spin silk and to build the house wherein it must die. By this house, when speaking of the soul, I mean Christ. I think I heard or read somewhere, either that our life is hid in Christ, or in God (which means the same thing), or that Christ is our life. It makes little difference to my meaning which of these quotations is correct …

Forward then, my daughters! Hasten over your work and build the little cocoon. Let us renounce self-love and self-will, care for nothing earthly, do penance, pray, mortify ourselves, be obedient, and perform all the other good works of which you know. Act up to your light; you have been taught your duties. Die! Die as the silkworm does when it has fulfilled the office of its creation, and you will see God and be immersed in His greatness, as the little silkworm is enveloped in its cocoon. Understand that when I say, 'you will see God', I mean in the manner described, in which He manifests Himself in this kind of union.

Now let us see what becomes of the 'silkworm', for all I have been saying leads to this. As soon as by means of this prayer the soul has become entirely dead to the world, it comes forth like a lovely little white butterfly! Oh, how great God is! How beautiful is the soul after having been immersed in God's grandeur and united closely to Him for but a short time! Indeed, I do not think it is ever so long as half an hour. Truly, the spirit does not recognise itself, being as different from what it was as is the white butterfly from the repulsive caterpillar. It does not know how it can have merited so great a good, or rather, whence this grace came which it well knows it merits not. The soul desires to praise our Lord God and longs to sacrifice and die a thousand deaths for Him. It feels an unconquerable desire for great crosses and would like to perform the most severe penances; it sighs for solitude and would have everyone know God, while it is bitterly grieved at seeing them offend Him. These matters will be described more fully in the next mansion; there they are of the same nature, yet in a more advanced state the effects are stronger, because, as I told you if, after the soul has received these favours, it strives to make still further progress, it will experience great things.

—*The Fifth Mansion*
from *The Interior Castle, chapter 2, nos. 2 –7*
The Life of Saint Teresa, tr. J. M. Cohen, Penguin

FURTHER READING

FURTHER READING

Books, 1957.

The Complete Works of St Teresa of Jesus, tr. & ed.
E. Allison Peers, Sheed & Ward, 1946.

The Letters of St Teresa of Jesus, 2 vols, tr.
E. Allison Peers, Sheed & Ward, 1951.

Auclair, Marcelle, *St Teresa of Avila,* Burns &
Oates, 1953.

Burrows, Ruth, *Interior Castle Explored,* Sheed &
Ward, 1981.

Byrne, Lavinia, *Traditions of Spiritual Guidance,*
Cassell, 1990.

Francis of Osuna, *The Third Spiritual Alphabet,*
Toledo, 1527.

Hamilton, Elizabeth, *The Great Teresa,* Chatto &
Windus, 1960.

Hoornaert, R., *Saint Teresa in her Writings,*
tr. J. Leonard, Sheed & Ward, 1931.

Peers, E. Allison, *Mother of Carmel,* SCM Press,
1945.

Peers, E. Allison, *Studies of the Spanish Mystics,*
SPCK, 1951.

Peers, E. Allison, *Saint Teresa of Jesus,* Faber &
Faber, London, 1953.

Sackville-West, V., *The Eagle and the Dove,*
Michael Joseph, 1943.

St John of the Cross, *Poems,* tr. Roy Campbell,
Penguin Classics, 1960.

Walsh, William Thomas, *Saint Teresa of Avila,*
    Bruce Publishing Company, Milwaukee,
    1943.

Weber, Alison, *Teresa of Avila and the Rhetoric of
    Feminity,* Princeton University Press, New
    Jersey, 1990.

Williams, Rowan, *Teresa of Avila,* Geoffrey
    Chapman, 1991.

Also in the 'Saints Alive' series

AUGUSTINE OF HIPPO

Augustine was the first modern man, someone who wrote out his own story in his *Confessions*, who wrestled to understand his motivation, his dreams and the life of the unconscious. He fathered an illegitimate son, and then, on his conversion, abandoned the child's mother. He took risks, trying out different life styles until he found the one which worked for him. He dared to ask questions of God and of his own experience, grappling with the truth. The life of Augustine was troubled and fascinating, and his questions honest and uncompromising.